SCAR

Also by Bruce Bond

Choreomania

The Calling

Words Written Against the Walls of the City

Plurality and the Poetics of Self

Frankenstein's Children

Rise and Fall of the Lesser Sun Gods

Dear Reader

Blackout Starlight: New and Selected Poems: 1997-2015

Sacrum

Gold Bee

Immanent Distance: Poetry and the Metaphysics of the Near at Hand

Black Anthem

For the Lost Cathedral

The Other Sky

Choir of the Wells

The Visible

Peal

Blind Rain

Cinder

The Throats of Narcissus

Radiography

The Anteroom of Paradise

Independence Days

SCAR

Bruce Bond

etruscan press

Etruscan Press
Wilkes University
84 West South Street
Wilkes-Barre, PA 18766
(570) 408-4546

 Wilkes
University

www.etruscanpress.org

Published 2020 by Etruscan Press
Printed in the United States of America
Cover image: *Transmission* © Aron Wiesenfeld
Cover design by Mickey Leonard
Interior design and typesetting by Julianne Popovec
The text of this book is set in Bembo.

First Edition

17 18 19 20 5 4 3 2 1

Library of Congress Cataloguing-in-Publication Data

Names: Bond, Bruce, 1954- author.
Title: Scar / Bruce Bond.
Description: First edition. | Wilkes-Barre, PA : Etruscan Press, 2020.
Identifiers: LCCN 2019015957 | ISBN 9781733674140 (pbk. : acid-free paper)
Classification: LCC PS3552.O5943 A6 2020 | DDC 811/.54--dc23
LC record available at https://lccn.loc.gov/2019015957

Please turn to the back of this book for a list of the sustaining funders of Etruscan
Press.

This book is printed on recycled, acid-free paper.

CONTENTS

Acknowledgements

The author would like to thank the editors of the following journals where poems from this book formerly appeared: *Asheville Poetry Review, American Journal of Poetry, Birmingham Poetry Review, Blackbird, Brilliant Corners, The Classical Outlet, Cloudbank, Dialogist, Florida Review, Hayden's Ferry Review, Hopkins Review, Laurel Review, Literary Matters, Pleiades, Plume, Quarterly West, South Coast Poetry Journal, Southern Review, The Sunflower Collective, The Writer's Garret,* and *Willow Springs.*

SCAR

I.

Here, to the ripple cut by the cold, drifts this
Bird, the long throat bent back, and the eyes in hiding.

—Louise Bogan

THE LOST LANGUAGE

1.

The concertina of the post-war ghetto
begs the question. Who are we deceiving.
The ping of the banjo and lone snare
speak a foreign tongue, and we know them
as speechless, and still they speak, still
they open the broken windows of Prague
to take it in. Concertina, I am lost.
When you walk the tenements at dawn,
longing to be useful, what good are accents
of the wooden leg in the promenade.
And in the aftermath, when music ends,
how come we hear you still. And we call
you *ravenous* or *con* or *unrepaired*.
We call you *refugee* and hold you near.

2.

When the pianist closes her eyes,
hands across the breakage of the keys,
I wonder, does it bring her any closer.
Half a life, I'm told, consists of signs,
but the other half has no pretense
of remaining. The path ahead is dark
as records were when I was a kid,
alone, and I could not hear my parents.
I fell in love to this. I closed my eyes.
Why must the flesh of angels be a song.
Is the harp-like hand more memorable,
if not eternal. Like the hush of the wake
behind our craft, as the searchlight dims,
and a green across the breakers lingers.

3.

When I was too young to remember,
I had no name. I was alone in paradise.
I know this, but who am I, too old to call
back the hands that carried me to bed.
I call that world *my* world, and when I talk
the world calls me *you*, in my mother's
worried voice. Her hand on my forehead,
her scolding, her twitch, the thankless chores,
they worry my words before I speak them.
My world before I had a world was scared
and pushed a face ahead to bear the blow.
When I was forgotten, or feared as much,
I woke. Without the language yet, I breathed.
I wept pure music would not be consoled.

4.

When language was mere madrigal and cry,
I must have heard the waters of the nameless
exceed the limits of the shore. Or felt
my own inarticulate want addressed
or turned away, my fears exhumed, expelled.
I felt and did not feel, as hands do
their coffees and their cigarettes. They feel
and do not feel the emptiness in them,
or some anonymous abundance spilling
over. When language was music alone,
I dreamt that I was two people, one known,
the other beside a window in the rain.
And it was beautiful, the rain, back when
it had nothing to do with sadness. Or rain.

5.

In the beginning, there was no number
one, not as the ancients fathomed it.
To be numbered, language needed two
or more taken as one. A conversation.
At two, we were just beginning to speak
to them, and to the others, this one, that.
Every voice, a little song. I am told,
when I first heard music, I heard no
numbers, then I did. I listened close
to count the footsteps in my fourths, fifths,
the odd sums that could not be broken
and be a music still. They moved me.
The many numbers in any one, the one
rapture in the many, speechless and alone.

6.

These days, the town lies restless, old,
and busy getting older, getting *there*.
The wrecking ball makes an ecstasy
of brick, the dust rises, the smoke subsides.
It's here I looked down at my body
and found it was not mine after all,
but more a house I rented, the beaten-down
palace of my youth, alive with ghosts
of old lovers, friends. If you touch this,
it tremors still. It shivers back to life
like a bird inside a sorcerer's pocket.
She was my first. And I moaned *God*
or *Sandy* without thinking. In the moment
of our union, I was broken in two.

7.

When ashes fall, the word for ashes falls
a little later. *Little,* I say, in deference
to a moment whose margins are enormous.
The measure of an arrow at the speed
of light is not its end. I confine myself
to earth, however deadly here, because
the skies are lovely. They breathe. Every time
I speak the word *breadth,* it comes out
breath. So much of love is obvious:
spouse, cats, the colors of our particular dawn
fading in the sea. Somewhere are the names
my mother taught me, though I cannot tell
you whose are whose. *She is in there,* I say,
alone, afraid. *Blue, black, phosphorescent.*

8.

Light falls from the sky to glass to table,
and we call it one light, across the faces,
one blaze that has no face. I have heard
that music is a language. It is. It is not.
The more specific I am, the more music
I lose. The more general I am, likewise.
Music is a language in the way the cries
of wolves are, and not, and cannot be
torn from their occasion. Instinct makes
their voices general, their pain specific,
their echo large. I think therefore I am
standing before a canyon. I am small.
The cant of two in one is everywhere,
the blade of *is* that cuts the bread of light.

9.

When I first saw Earth from a distance,
I was told the marble stood for one
world, and I was standing on an icon,
although I could not see it without help.
It must have been the dark around it
that made this little lamp so priceless,
as eyes are, and the skies they gather,
the black in them that dwindles to a star.
My mother told me once, do not worry.
You are young. You have a long life
ahead. No need for a child to dwell
on such things. It helped. And then it didn't.
It taught me. When children ask about
death, they must be speaking of their own.

10.

Our first world, before we understood
the world as first, or ours, or there to wander
and explain; it never left completely,
never abandoned what we think about
and how, although it feels far away,
nameless, as rivers meeting oceans are,
or particles waves, a child the lion
of homes on fire, bereft of words to meet them.
Our first world is there, as silence is
in the invitation to speak, abstention
in the glass through which the daylight falls.
Our word *mother* materialized through
a hole in the air that was motherless,
although her absence calls to us as ours.

11.

If you are searching for a friend online,
an insomniac to break the bread
of misery and silence, look no farther.
Trust me, says anonymous, *the voice*
in rivers after dark is no illusion.
It is an angel. And who can resist.
If I am broken just enough, I fly.
I suspend my physical heart, alive,
among the saints and champion banners.
I never met an angel, but I saw one
once in a painting, in one hand poppies,
the other a harp, and though it made no music,
it seemed so finely strung in the fire
of a child's hair, it nearly played itself.

12.

The spiders in the skeletons of lamps
and castles that burned down years ago,
they die, and die again, and I hear them
in silence, see them in their silent labor.
In a garden made of ashes, they weave
what spiders call *many veins in the eye*
of God, or, *Bach's Partita in d Minor,*
and on and on. I cannot remember.
I have heard that music is a vast web.
Each note has a measure of the one
before and after, thus the threads beyond
number, and the air that flexes through.
And when music ends, the web goes still.
As faces do. Lit by a house in flames.

13.

The pause before the opening measure
of the string quartet plays a theme
whose variations fall between the movements.
At every door, the scent of April snow,
the memory of a man who slept badly,
if at all. He will tell you, when times are
hard, music calls the way silence does
the prisons of the north. On his desk,
the Jewish prayers he set to music. He
opens a drawer, having scored them
for that particular dark. It made them
darker, more particular, less bound.
It made prayer a space to hide the beauty
of his anger, as he slid the music in.

14.

The music of the gifted few, chosen
to survive, brings no comfort here.
Can you blame the prisoner in line
to face the chambers, if he curses, spits,
turns away. Whatever the tearful
waltz or anthem, it cannot see you.
It has no eyes. The birds above the ash
factories remind you, music has no
pity, its call no rival, its acolyte no code.
It has no power to barter or explain.
And if the commandant hums along,
he hums alone. And if he weeps, he weeps
for no one. Or a little of everything,
and a lot of nothing. Nothing at all.

15.

The first world is hostile. Like the last.
Or so I imagine. The path, the passing.
If I plant a garden there, I am not alone.
Every autumn, the harps of alders lay
bare their strings and shred the wind to ribbons.
I do not know when beauty first scared me.
Or made me small and large. All at once.
When I saw the sky turn to flocks of sheep
above the Angeles Crest, I could not quite
fit them in my eyes. I want to say
my first storm was grievous in its glory,
the first trees swept by a greater power.
I want to say the breezes gathered them
to let them fall. To whisper of the falling.

16.

Long ago I cried. I spat. I breathed.
The shock of arrival kicked my heart
to life and the will to make it known.
Everybody suffers. And it is good
to know, when I look at your face,
I see a scorch of blood beneath the surface.
Long ago a teacher taught me to read
in each the occasion of its fate. She
said it would make me more patient,
sentient, kind, less vulnerable to anger.
And so, I did. I died. I died again.
When I was little and love leaned in,
I was not prepared. My second shock
was this. The stifled cry, my second word.

17.

Whatever I hear in the wordless song,
I cannot find the words. Whoever you are,
thank you. Where would I be without you.
And you, dear painting without narrative,
or fable without epilogue, dear world
without end. Whatever I am, I am
always on the threshold. Out of the earth
and back. My father's ashes were a lot
like this, and as they left, they left a place
no one spoke of. They had the gravity
of wisdom. But they were never wise.
They had a name and were nameless still.
Like the plentitude before a word
and after, the part that rises up and over.

18.

Every home is the one I lost to fire.
When I speak of it, I have two homes,
one of which is missing. When I speak
of fire, it climbs the darkness like a church.
It lowers a ladder for smoke to escape,
angels to descend. I have two fears.
I have two passions. The past and its passing.
For years I hid the terror of the burning
doors that forged me, transported me,
until my dreams had little more to say.
But just last night, I asked the startled child,
which boy are you. And a look of wonder
took the place of fear. It wiped the slate.
And the mist of chalk whispered: *darker.*

19.

To the face inside my face, I ask,
where is the light that beat you all those years.
Where the little plastic phonograph,
the toy car, the lion with one eye.
Back when I woke to my missing half,
I could hear down the hall in the night:
a spoon, a bowl, the chime of a hunger
that never goes away. My father said
if I chant the number one in my head,
the doors of dream will open, and they did.
Once. Why is it our peaceful number
is likewise the most paranoid and dull.
Save when it is canted, sung, at one
with its passing, one minus one minus one.

20.

When I want a thing, I put a little
music in my voice. It comes by instinct,
the hunger in the song before it is sung,
and so, I imagine, it never goes away.
A new language comes out of no one
person or place and a little of the all.
When I think of my father, I think
of words turning into water. I think,
therefore I stream his music in my head.
My measure of him phrased, desired, mourned.
Hard to resurrect the world without
a world left out, to make our losses sing.
Where there is one, there must be two.
I too am scared. Paradise is lonely.

21.

If I could talk to an angel I could trust,
I would say, I think you know my friend
who had no stomach for the talking cure.
If I exorcize my demons, so go my angels,
he said. Call it a mere figure of speech,
and you break the glass of figurines
songs are made of. It is a figure. There.
I confess. I grow weary of these songs
that tear the heart from its closet and wing it
out so far from earth each singer is alone.
If I could talk to my friend who had his
demons, I would. If I could raise the tremor
of our cups. (*Are you free for breakfast, I
cannot sleep.*) If I knew how serious it was.

22.

A song is not a flock, however much
each solo has a little of the plural,
a lot of none, a touch of the body
immersed in the common element,
as the faithful are in a local river,
at one with the father and yet no god.
If you are lost, you are not alone.
Music walks the waters of the world
in search of those who are already here.
One lies down with the lion of each
and sighs as lovers do and heavy objects.
Nights lie down in rivers that are restless
as grief we cannot talk about right now.
So fierce the pins of stars against the water.

23.

If ever I fly alone, I talk with strangers
or not at all, and stranger later is how
it matters more than I know, what it is
I grant, in some unmeasured fashion,
the note of kind regard or condescension,
passing, as music does, into a general
pattern of which I am a part. I tell
myself our paths will never cross again,
and so I board the plane, undistracted
by the sound of friends and the familiar
names, prone to disappear, as folks do
into the general pattern I call the world,
the one that does not know me, by name,
or where a stranger takes me when she goes.

24.

About now the conversation has turned
political, which makes even the most
egregious bore at the party feel a little
anxious, a slave to the glass he empties
and fills, because there is just so much
room for error and smoke and cruel
behavior behind the curtain, and the fire
that is the subject of our conference panel
has people in it and therefore silence,
and therefore, the politics of the room
bespeaks a more generalized concern,
more plagued than reported, more full
of emptiness as water is to those who
plunge, hand in hand, and cannot hear a word.

25.

To every temple, its panoply of idols
where spirits lie. I said this to a flag
once with a coffin beneath the shadow
flag below. It was time. I was told.
It was not personal. I dipped my head
in silent grace and looked up, drenched.
To every stately office, a pride of columns.
I loved my country with my good hand
across my heart. *Under God,* I said,
because I was told. It was time. After
all, I too feared death, and loved earth
movers and gods of similar proportions.
I was small in the sky, as flags are small
in the pointless wind that makes them fly.

26.

When the speeches end, and music begins
to frame a better argument for listening,
balloons fall out of the convention hall
ceiling, and the candidate and family
hold up their hands, so audible the cheer,
no one can hear the lyrics, let alone
one's own strange voice inside the voices.
Here beneath the happy spheres of air
bouncing on our heads, hope surrenders
what it can to the gala that never parts
a curtain, the throb of lower registers
more felt than heard, more willfully suppressed,
crushed, as fury is inside the earth,
beneath the smoke and thunder of the crowd.

27.

Here we are again in a market square
where no one lives, on the street where malls
go to die, the air conditioners frozen,
halls blind, the atoms among the atoms
gone spiritual, as Pythagoras imagined.
The body and soul of the harmonium,
the monochord, the mode, they spin stars
and starlets still. Songs-turned-disc-turned-
digital-file, they turn up everywhere,
encrypted, stolen, shared. There is nothing
pure about music. So much of heaven
is free-access now, so yes, musicians
suffer, but music. Music says, *whatever,*
unburdening its pockets, breath by breath.

28.

What I am trying to say, I cannot say
without a sense of failure and the will
to fail again. I was born in a nation
I could not fathom. *Love it*, they said,
and I fell silent, hand above my heart.
When I hid beneath my desk, the bomb
I heard above me had my name on it.
My name in another's handwriting.
My name on the notebook of a girl
nearby who made me equally uneasy.
I held my knees the way lovers hold
each other in the movies, how they listen
in their shelter for the thrum of planes
and violins to drown their hidden passions.

29.

Isn't every language a little lost.
Lost as in *a child at the zoo,* or
wagers lost, or *a boat without oars*
in a sea of music. Lost, as *songs*
are lost to the air that made them.
The voice of the beast in the bag
of me, it is in there, in the language
and its need to speak the cry before
I pour my expectations in. Each want
displaced, as water is, when we go in.
Who are the chosen if not immersed
in the light of the new world order,
our guardian a god, a father made
small at the cradle, to hear his name.

30.

The timer on the grand piano keeps
chipping at the stone of silence, and still
the silence is no smaller, form no less
the open invitation that it was.
Inside every box, the ever smaller,
the cough, the shoe, the car, and so on.
And then it is over. Glass dissolves.
The old world comes tumbling in.
What you feel in the supermarket
music is not music, but then you hear
in the air-conditioned timbre, the soul
who played it, arranged it, paid for it.
You hear the note of the dead still
abandoned life. Growing ever larger.

31.

When the art of the listening admits
a need to see its likeness in the woods,
the mating calls of birds take on a note
of grief whose anonymities are yours,
your loss unspecific, your species lost,
your cry to be chosen light as air.
The music knows something about me
I cannot know. Or it says as much,
then it fades. And I want to follow
but not too close. Mystery is a measure
of why I come, listen, why these nerves
subside when a sense of form emerges.
First one bird. Then by design, another,
and in their rapture, all of April answers.

32.

Nervous breakdowns of the dissolute
or meticulous obsessive know a thing
about *form* and *chaos* that makes it
hard to talk. Hard to turn the water
into wine when you are drowning. If
only it were simple. We would say
the words *exclusion, empire, madness,*
without thinking of the hospice garden.
What I want for the sad and nervous
is a book of psalms, the kind you read
backwards, if you choose, if you invent
your path. Just maybe you read it twice.
Maybe the last page is blank as light,
as doors that open as you close your eyes.

33.

The widow prepares for bed, again,
same pills, creams, same movable teeth,
same emptiness beside her on one
side of the bed, a radio on the other.
Long ago her forebears carved a flute
from the bone of a bird, and thereby
came together, listened, and survived.
When I read the new dark argument
for this form or that, I think of this:
the pill, the book, the tribe beside the fire.
Inside the bird-made-flute, an emptiness.
Inside me, no less. And inside that,
a bird. It has been dead a long time now.
The wound in each is endlessly resourceful.

34.

Follow the feral kids and factories
down the shores of Houston after dark,
and you come to the place floodlight climbs
the tall smoke to make of it a palisade
of progress, and in the crumpled-car lot,
a man sets fire to a dumpster, and out
of nowhere, a stranger, and then another,
and moths of eyes come a little closer.
A cigarette changes hands, and talk
follows, and sometimes a quiet hmm
implies, I am listening, nothing more.
Not much, but sometimes it is enough
like a breath beside you in the dark,
its music borne on the dying portion.

35.

I have a name for death, but God knows
what it means. I have words for a lot
of things that crumble when you touch them.
More and more talk at the funeral home
marks the grave of its occasion. I visit.
I think. The other name for forget-
me-nots is scorpion grass. Me, I like
both at once. Make that all the words,
all colors in this spectacle of white.
My friend for whom language touches all,
he had a name. As he said, a ticket
to gain admission, recognition, love.
When he died, he had it still. He who
left with nothing at all. He had a name.

36.

I read a man who spoke on behalf
of things that cried out to him and to his
language to preserve them. Silly things.
Each longed to be flotsam of the shore
survivors kneel to read. Call us readers
waves then, and every day we pour
over what remains of one night's wreck.
We commit our loved ones to the deep
and endless regress of suns gone down
and never quite abandoned. Tell me.
How credible is any sentiment now,
laid in stone, without the providence
of strangers. How impossible and far
the seagull's cry without the salt that stings.

37.

I loved a stranger once I did not see
as strange, and she returned the blindness.
Together we turned the radio up,
powered all the windows down and drove.
Music was ahead of its time back then,
before I knew it would be, as it is.
I was taught it was wrong to love myself.
My lover told me, and I believed her.
It was the beginning of the end.
When I think of her, I am parked, past
curfew, on a fire-break at the edge
of the arroyo, calling to her home.
Emptiness makes my voice a little larger,
and larger still, the emptiness replies.

38.

When I was a child, I dug a hole
big enough to lie in, and I spoke
to it. I told it what I could not tell
the others, how my father hit me,
and my friend, and the world I smashed
my bike in. And I hit myself back,
so I would never crash again. At first
I was the victim in each story, but
the hole knew better. It knew I had
to forget now and then, to lie even,
to spare the self I made. But also, I
had to leave some gift, so I gave it all
the suffering I, a child, could, and rose,
like a heart inside a surgeon's hands.

39.

No end to interpretation, my professor
said as if his *no* were the permission
slip we, his students, would now hold out
for his autograph, and I know I am
a little mean and young without end.
Not that I disagree, or fear the boundless
as some might fear a deadline or dad,
only that the story of words like *never*
begins a bit earlier, closer to nothing,
every time, so I go back, to the Gothic
ni for *no,* and *aiwi* meaning *vital force,*
like the wind inside the word, which began
before memory or speech, one body
cut from another, to breathe the mystery in.

40.

I dreamt my cat slept across my thigh,
her head on my knee, and when she woke,
the world appeared to her no different
than a moment ago, when she dreamt.
No less nameless, our eyes. *Our selves,* she said.
Believe me. I had my doubts as well.
Half the time she talks, all I hear is music.
All she wants is music in return.
Then I woke up. And I had no cat.
Not that cat. It had been years now.
And the world appeared as it was
a moment ago, but silence was thicker,
loss a presence, a feeling of too much,
a radiant surge taking back the shore.

II.

But here the dark
has been stolen in a sack
weighted down with a pebble
and drowned.

—John Berger

SCAR

1.

I came into this world through a tear
in the fabric, and still it was one world
to gather, mend, one afterbirth, one mother
christened in the wreckage of her labor.
She had a name, my father's name, in mine.
She had a birth trauma of her own,
but the first cry came from a nameless place.
It was nothing personal. Our cry.
You and I were born to be born again
through a cleft in the air between us.
Whatever the precedent, tell me, is it
any darker than our breathing now.
We were cut. From the one. We are,
says breath, the cut of the one we were.

2.

Today I catch sight of the scar my student
pulls the cuff of her sleeve to conceal,
and she answers a look I did not know
I gave her. *I was*, she tells me, *working
through some issues,* and she hands me
a poem. *I'm so sorry*, I say, in proxy
for a mystery. I want to say more.
Then less. I am pulling at a sleeve
of my own. *It's fine*, she says. *Writing
helps,* and so I read, I cut. I question.
How deep is too deep. I do not know.
Is the knife still there. Does it move
as the eye moves, asleep, the page gone dark,
the lid in shivers. Asking to be raised.

3.

When the skin breaks, the pupil flares.
It blackens with the light that is one
part particle, another wave, another
a lens wept over the aperture, a portal,
a pore, to make a startled bloodstream rise.
It could be a feed from the other side
of hell, the wounded leg of a child
fresh from the minefield, and we wince
at the opening, not knowing whose.
What I see I am seeing at a distance.
Wherever I go, I go. I cast a shadow,
a glance, a wave against the shattering
stones of shore. Call it what you will.
Half of every testament is broken.

4.

A cutter cuts. Then, she stops. She heals.
She calls herself *a cutter*. For how long,
I cannot say. The scar she bears runs
deep into the shadow of the sleeve.
Deep as wolves in a hamlet of snow,
the dark that makes a seer of the seen.
A cutter disappears from the silence
of a family meal. What she cuts, she cuts
into friends, an accordion of dolls.
You out there. If you are truly alone,
what is there to fear. *Pinch me*, says
the bewildered at dawn. *Am I dreaming*.
She knows. This sensation could be her
dream, or not. What difference does it make.

5.

I knew a girl who was sick so often,
her family told her it was *in her head*.
Turned out, it was. *Blame it on the brain,*
she said, as if it were a thing apart,
as waters are from the names of rivers.
I remember how her knees gave out,
her eyes rolled back, her one hand
clawed the air, and the teacher said,
You, get the nurse. Do not touch her.
Give her air. So we gave her nothing.
We gathered just so close, never closer,
and watched, afraid of the stifled voice,
her tongue's muscle like an arm, half-way
down her throat, our heads half-angled away.

6.

I have a friend who *saw things* and wrote
them down for no one in particular,
so furious and desperate the pages
of her poems caught fire. Each night
in a turkey roaster. She made sure.
She turned her work over to the cinders.
It helped. I cannot say I understand.
Slowly she got better. *All the best poems,*
she said, *turn to ashes.* Sooner or later.
All the best dreams burn the fuel of day.
Of course, there was a note of grief in that.
Heard or imagined. There was a hole,
full of echoes. And it broke her cry
into ever smaller, more merciful cries.

7.

Eighty-four months in the Hanoi Hilton,
and my father's cousin never broke,
although he suffered burns and deprivations
that made his face a mask. He even beat
himself to spite the Vietcong cameras.
He even slit his wrists. So when the war
dumped its copters in the sea, he returned,
a cripple, indebted to the art of holding
back. I barely knew him, in his corner
chair, his eyes on the floor, mine on him.
Was there something he wanted tell us
as our knives dug in. Did small talk make
him feel more included. More left out.
What more did I, a free man, have to say.

8.

To every tower, its vertigo. No stone
can pin us down. It is not the ground
alone that scares us. It is the triumph
of the high-rise moving in next door,
the nervous pride that makes ours obsolete.
I lived in my father's shadow once
back when I thought he could not die.
When he left, his shadow cut right through.
When I hear an hour break into bells,
I look up, as if his ghost were near,
and the tolling here were somewhere far.
If I relish feeling small, praise be
the beneficence of giants, their flesh
the resurrected shadow of a child.

9.

When my cousin came home in a box,
I said a prayer. I did it for him, I said.
I made a beautiful tower of my lies
and lay beneath the shadow where I,
forever, slept. One day, I said, my nation
will crumble into the sun or worse.
My holy cross will sink into its shadow.
Each love set down in Veterans Park
will echo *I am the narrow gate*, but you,
cousin, you will survive. The cigarette
in your lips will flutter back to the flame.
As it was, it will be. I will be clueless.
And you talk rarely, if at all, haloed
in smoke. Like the stars of Vietnam.

10.

Tombs in rows will tell you: the dead
are soldiers still. We pay respects, like debt,
to give them a place in the larger order.
Call uniformity a gift to the widow
grown small now in the arms of a boy.
Call it war. But do not call it progress.
If history comes from the hills to hunt,
it is a dream, and dreams end, though no one
knows where. *I'll tell you a story*, says
a mother to the child who never knew
his father. Can you blame the kid if he
sees himself there. *Let me tell you*, she says,
and together they enter a cloud of ash.
Together they pull a stranger from the fire.

11.

The architecture of capitols and church
estates raises a wave against the eye,
and we call the proportions *tidal,*
the stones *classic* or *gothic* or the new
sublime. If the whole of the ocean
prepared an edifice to meet the shore,
rest assured, it would have a crest
like this, the gravity of some great thing,
a swell descending, never breaking down.
I wounded my mother when I arrived,
as she did me when she departed. I
entered a tall emptiness that made me
as small as my voice was large. As if.
Abandonment were power. And value, law.

12.

Poppies fall asleep and fade, although
the word remains, then falls, a little later.
It enters the circle of another genus,
another vase. When I read, I feel it:
the full-blown field flustered in its plumage.
A stem of sunlight slips through the crystal,
a gaze slips through the seer in the seen,
and we give the whole a flower's title.
Any wonder we grace our hospitals
in meadows. Or a field of blossoms looks
to the harvest blade to consecrate
their light. The colors of grief burn in them.
Against the resting place we give them.
The smoke that falls against each chiseled name.

13.

Where did it come from, this paradise.
I have read that book. It was a gift.
It made clear no light before this light.
Only a ghost economy of gifts.
It was confusing. God who had no body
yet, looks down on us, His speculum,
and we give back an image of the flesh
whose death is ours alone. I hated it
when my father died, and a friend stood
at the ceremony, his head in a heaven
that had—as he saw it—my father in it.
But I had no father. I had a brother.
And he looked at me that moment as if
to say, *Who the hell does he think he is.*

14.

I knew a boy in college who shook a lot
when he got high, and when he quit cold,
he broke down. So I was told. He vanished.
He swore, years later, at a far away bar,
God brought us together, God who needle-
and-threads our broken pieces like a surgeon.
Then he pulled out a clipping on the shroud
of Turin, something he carried in his shirt,
and I knew I did not know him well.
He had found *something*. And talked real
quick, his glass overflowing, the battered
newsprint of his savior held up once more.
Proof positive we were the birds of Christ,
and it fluttered in his disappointed hand.

15.

The journey feels unlikely with coincidence
and fate, and yet whatever confidence
spins us through the great design remains
a little nervous. I barely think of it.
Earth's demise is something I write off.
Like a nightmare or vascular condition.
Sunlight comes and goes and goes. Who here
is any less compulsive. Do the extremities
of alignment and disorder describe, for you,
two candidates for a bad day. Lucky me.
My cat is funny. Nothing means nothing
to her. She eats. She plays. She eats the hand
that feeds her. *Just kidding*, she says, *I'd never
do that.* And then. By accident, she does.

16.

What I recall starts mid–stream, ankle-deep
in the clouds of summer, and another boy
just beaned me with a stone to the head.
An accident. I thought. And then he ran.
It seemed so innocent. Our game of stones.
The plunk and shatter of the stream no sooner
broken than repaired. That said, I never
knew a rock could raise an ache that deep,
a betrayal that uncertain, a sphere of blood
that bold. I never saw the boy again.
He took with him the end of a story
that just goes on, as streams do, and vague
sensations, and the shadows of boys grown
tall at dusk, somewhere in these mountains.

17.

I used to think all of my experience
laid its tracks in the snow, and one day,
I would go there. I would lay a footprint
in each footprint as snow does in the snow.
I was cruel to a toad—I see him still—
a puppet I made sing with my hands.
I was cruel, I was cruel, says a voice
in the winter stars. Some days the cant
is mine alone, which is no less odd
and beautiful, to think the longing to be
better is snow filling up with snow.
Other days I believe in one great mind,
somewhere out there. Over here, I call.
Follow my voice, I say. My hands, I sing.

18.

Cut with sunlight and magnifying glass
this leaf, and you are a child like me.
Fry this ant in a rosary of ants,
and I am your friend. Bound by shame,
together we are strangers to ourselves,
our regrets. What is light if not late.
Take these stars, indebted to the dark
that makes one shine, another fearful,
and a third, in frozen light, a god.
The hatred of my colleague for my friend
confessed to me late, in tears, weeks
after he died. *Late.* As the dead are late.
She hated him no less, and still she wept.
I never knew just who she cried for.

19.

Once I threw a stone at a bird and missed.
I was no god, and so I spared us both.
I was cruel and tried to give my cruelty
away. Here, I said, to the branches, here.
Every god I cared about was mortal
and therefore dangerous. In search of me,
my rock, the blood of the parable
that never came to life. I wrote a paper
on *Heart of Darkness* when I was far
too young, looking for a story to tell
the story, dirt to expurgate the dirt.
Hell, I thought, the heart was black enough.
Or was the planet dark, the heart in it
clenched about the hard part, like an eye.

20.

After he returned from death, the man,
according to his gospel, held out his hand
before the skeptical eye of his disciple,
and the lesion there, however closed,
proved to be the more powerful claim.
Thus the doubter felt ashamed, pointless
as it was, the disavowal of his reason.
And the dead man said, *Don't be so hard.*
Love the stubborn stone of your skull
as you do your neighbor. I doubt death
speaks to me. But then, one night, pain
arrives, holds out its hands. So I make
for it a bed, boil milk, draw shade, so if
it dreams, it dreams it never wakes again.

21.

The scar on my brow was a third eye
once, and I gave the stranger my wallet,
and he took with it my school ID.
Just why he cut me, I will never know.
I was such a tiny motherfucker
and a motherfucker's precious stone,
and though the cut was just minor then,
it ran into the cradle of my eye.
It will always be that small, this cut.
It will always flinch at the stiletto
click of branches broken in the wind.
When I open a lamp, I open a well.
When I close, it closes, and the well
of light, because it is abandoned, grows.

22.

Tender regions of the brain take shelter
in the dark gone cold to keep them tender
like the windows of a house in the woods
in a purity of night apart from others.
I had a friend whose mother ended it all
on his small bed when he was off at school.
Then he slept on it for weeks. Imagine.
He was good enough to me, I guess,
but aloof from his lovers. His mother slept
among them all. It made him special,
to speak with such odd calm about pain
as someone well acquainted with this subject.
If he cried, he did not recall. If a smell
troubled his sleep, sleep alone would tell.

23.

Say we shatter October into shadows,
sparrows, spills across the workshop floor,
and the child you see sees his father
lay down the unruly hammer and curse.
In an instant, the father hides his anguish.
The boy is young, too young to know much
about his limits. Where a child ends,
the long suppression of our pain begins.
Animal, corruptible, alchemical as fire,
the name for human damage is somewhere.
When I look now at the man, his eyes
look back in shame. Let me begin again.
It is October. Everywhere the leaves
of shadow fall, in flames, to earth and through.

24.

When I come from the wilderness,
I come alone. I could not learn this
from the pastorals of prayer. The god
who dies when a childhood dies fells
a father's body. Only then is death
a hammer. Its one eye looks down on us.
The god who once survived his death is
not as visible now. Or breakable,
personal, though his suffering bears
the burden. It gets confusing to a kid,
the one god who lives in our fathers.
I want to say they come to life in spaces
where we talk. You and I, face to face,
in the untouched light that has no face.

25.

As a boy, I dreamt I had another father.
He was somewhere on a beach in the sun
of Southern California. Look at me,
I said, the way dreams and scriptures do.
I had a happy life. Or so I imagined.
But my father was sad, or sadness was
how I understood his silence. All day
he read a book whose pages never turned.
Or they turned the way waves do, never
closer to the end. We were bound by that.
Look at me, I said, with my tiny shovel
and bright red pail. Every tower I built,
I built for you. Every dawn, a surge
reclaims the starlight clawing at the shore.

26.

When a bone breaks, it could be worse.
You could go numb with shock and say, *it could
be worse.* You might shiver from the jaws
of life, your heart gone racing in the wild.
The rubied beacon on the hook and ladder,
the medical mask, you see them now as props
in a movie where every victim is you. You
feel their pain and know it as theirs alone.
The sudden announcement of your ligament
and spleen, it stupefies. Sobers. Binds.
When a body breaks, a stranger comes forward
from the theater dark. The movie ends,
life begins. A man leans his face to yours
to ask. *How many fingers. What's your name.*

27.

I fed my pain to the irony machine,
and jewels of flies flew out the other side.
It was easy as breathing. It was a dream
without an ocean. A darkening below.
I too have a phony double, or two.
The irony machine is our robot friend.
It thumps the heart like a dusty carpet.
If a *metaphor* is a bearing over, where,
I ask. You who are listening, where.
I have heard you come and go like time's
device I take for granted until it breaks.
Know this. I want for you a better life.
Most cardinal when broken. Like ribs
that ache pure light in the gathering swells.

28.

The scar in my arm is the palest part,
thickest where most broken. What did I know:
I was just a kid and hated it, my whiteness,
and got a beating from a stranger who felt
the same. I held my tongue. It was all
about me: the guilt, the plea, the pointless
wind and its absolution in the leaves.
I read once, *To wound a soul is to create it.*
Do not believe it. The silence of our kids
bears witness. A million words for a stranger,
none of them battered or strange enough.
The bigger picture could be bigger, bolder.
The bell in the bayou. Red bronze of dawn.
The million silent children bathed in blood.

29.

The margins of the road home narrow
in the snow. I am not alone. I tell myself,
light is a feral creature. It hides, hunts,
feeds on the dark to see the half of it.
Long ago I lost the will to sleep.
So sleep came crashing through the crest of day.
I had wounds I did not know I had until
they opened. The sound of bells broke me
at the altar. I had gods who knelt and,
in perfect mercy, vanished, so I would not be
alone. I lost a friend, and silence came
in the breath that gathered and left. Untouched.
I lay in bed waiting. The flowers of winter
are blood. In the beginning, there was nothing.

30.

If I close the morning paper and let
the sunlight flood my breakfast, it is,
this day, in deference to the singing. So
visible the needle, so clear the thread,
so broken the news, there is no lyric in it.
Open, close, open, and out come birds,
the species never so specific, really.
Music tells us. To talk this way releases
a latch, and the breath in the cage lingers
a while before it flutters off, surprised.
The calliope of wings and petals says,
Beauty is singular. It has a body,
and so, a grave. And so brings comfort
to those who see it stumble out of earth.

31.

I was born in the middle of the night.
My mother told me. Scars in both of us
bear testament. She reminds me still.
Nights, late, in the season of her dotage,
she would call, afraid, her voice in splinters.
My head is spinning, do I take this pill.
And I saw birds making a nest of her hair
and tried to speak, to say the things that
songs say when the words have left them.
When I first learned to speak, I did not
make a sound. I became a residence
of tongues, some of which are lost. I learned
scar tissue breaks when I move. I move
to mend. I lie still to mend a little more.

32.

When I was lost, alone in the garden,
the doors of my house opened and closed
with no one there to hear. *Look at me,*
God, was the subtext of my prayer, so
I prayed some more. I made God personal,
the way one makes a promise at the bedside
of a child. And so we talked a while longer.
We walked into stories. We disappeared.
The long infection emptied my accounts,
and I took it as a sign. Of nothing.
Nothing, I thought, the moment of arrival,
nothing as we leave. When pain subsided,
it drew its smoke into my leg. I rose.
I walked and shivered lightly, like an eye.

33.

The face beneath your face is older, stranger,
crushed and battered, ready to emerge.
And under that, no face at all. I call it
childhood because I recollect so little,
and in my closet, when my mother died,
I found a skull I loved, phosphorescent
and therefore deadly, alive with whatever
shine it hoarded. It smelled of sulfur then,
like my great aunt who asked if I loved Jesus,
then held my hand in the bones of hers.
I feared her in ways I feared no death.
I was just a boy after all, my skull a toy.
And when it glowed, it shed the stuff of angels
and ice. Before a darkness took it back.

34.

Philosophers of the oneness of things
are philosophers no more. They mean
nothing without a breath to fill the sail
and travel elsewhere. Long ago, I walked
into a field, and I went missing. Poppies
bore the thorns of bees, and I named them.
If I stood still, I thought, the bees would
halo me as one of their own. I am not
special. Philosophers of oneness fill
theaters with tales where everything fits.
Everyone is special. Before my mother
died, she flew in dreams from the perch
of her spine to meet my father. She told
me. Twice. Her eyes blurred and shining.

35.

The fruit of human harvest is a scar. Look
down, and you look away. You mother calls,
she waits, one day she dies, and the chimes
of your closet take back their black jacket.
But there she is, where they cut you into life.
If I could talk serious of Eden, I would begin
with a scar, a cry turned darkest kindness
without creed. This is not a dream. Look up,
and you disappear, you answer, the wound
you wear pins you to your gut. In an Eden
of great surprise, panic turns to laughter.
Breathing gathers its flock. If you could see her,
this yard would tear its roots from earth and rise.
Then pause, suspended, tentacled, exposed.

36.

Where there is pain, there is confinement,
my chiropractor says. Ache cures ache,
breaking the adhesions, and I see stars.
I see a friend kicking his guitar case
from the stage, many years ago. He is
cursing his hands, and no one in the chapel
can talk him down. So powerful the clouds.
The tendons in his neck strain to keep
his head on. And us in class are looking
at each other, hunched, helpless, impatient.
Everywhere, the glory of his anger.
And at the bottom of that anger, shame.
At the bottom of this shame, more shame.
And everyone knew. Everybody felt it.

37.

The lonely have gone to their rooms again.
Alexa, put sleeping pills on the shopping list.
And every day is Christmas and a new box
if you stretch your means. The lonely have
mortgaged their loneliness because it's priceless.
Take all of it, I say. And still it grows.
I left three messages on my friend's machine
last month, because I'm alone, and his health
is a question, and his wife left for Europe.
It's fine, says the silence. *I love you. I'm good.*
Imagine how the machine feels. If you can,
you must be lonely. It understands nothing,
as if nothing were a friend. If it calls, it calls.
Don't worry. I'm good. Goodbye. I love you.

38.

The internet could crash any day now
and does, in nightmares of the solar flares
that last time set the telegraph on fire.
Science says, not *if,* but *when,* and planes
will fall, and the banks, and grids will sizzle.
Where there is design, there is a designer.
So said my father, when he was young.
It made sense the way beauty does not.
The thin wire of grief. Our litany of suns.
So much to learn and unlearn. To tear
from our systems with its small brass hooks.
I do know this. Sometimes at funerals,
the kinder sermon leaves providence alone.
So said my father. Long after he was gone.

39.

No birth into awareness without pain.
I read long ago, and it felt right enough
long before I suffered what it might have
meant, questioned it, and lost my faith.
Avoid the unlit streets, my mother said,
and so I walked off, if not into danger,
into suspicion. Rest assured. The past
is waiting, laid down in tears like a lens.
My mother loved me, bore me, bore with
my insufferable selfishness, my mewling
to be loved. But I can only be so fierce
before the lion of self-reproach walks out
of hiding. Then a bruise of dawn. It fades.
All dawns do it. Some of whom are nightmares.

40.

I sat very still for a day, then two.
For a week, then two, I sat. Waiting.
Month devoured month. Boredom
got more boring, until I was waiting,
I thought, no more. I was damaged,
my legs were on fire, but I expected,
I thought, nothing. And year by year,
the fire subsided. Smoke sank into my eyes.
Nothing arrived, as it will, as it does
each breath, and would never be the same.
But now and then, I feel a little something.
In storm season, when my stress is high,
my legs recall the season of my stillness.
In a time of stillness, the rainclouds fall.

III.

più lieve legno convien che ti porti

—Charon, Canto III

NARCISSUS IN THE UNDERWORLD

1.

Somewhere in the middle of my life,
in the shadow of towers that wall the street,
I turned, and in the traffic and the talk
and clash of horns in contrary motion,
someone called, but what I saw was no one.
Only the multitude, a hundred-some,
and the furious drifts of steam that rose
through grates of iron in the sidewalk.
There I was, confused in the general
havoc. I turned, the way death turns
a mirror to the wall, or a home to some
mausoleum of coats, hats, black umbrellas.
Somewhere in the middle of the night,
my brother called, and I became an orphan.

2.

Wherever I walked, I saw my father's face
across the face of a stranger. Then it left,
and the face grew stranger still. We were
all fathers and mothers then, with hearts
that knocked in us like angry neighbors.
Last night's dream was a black scarf falling,
fainting from a great height, the smooth
hands of its ephemera signing the air.
Once, when I could not sleep, the planet
opened, rubies ached in the gash like eyes,
and I, a child, entered. I walked against
a flume of steam; I looked, and some there
felt the rumble in their feet, some heard—
as I in passing heard—their own lost name.

3.

Then I was descending a flight of stairs
to take a chair at the internet café,
to join the others, heads bowed, ears wired,
mouthing messages to the no one there.
Can you hear me, someone asked, and so
I turned, listened, looked the other way.
The *great intellectual breeze* that moves
through all things, it moved. It withered.
I love that moment a stranger speaks in
your direction at someone on the other
side. You become, if not transparent,
a dark reflective surface. A bead of ink,
an open pupil. *Can you hear me,* asks
a voice somewhere, and *yes,* I say. *I can.*

4.

Hell has no guide, no message, no mouth,
no dead in flames as the dead imagined,
only these fetishes, rings, movies, blogs,
and you can go there. You can download
Tor and put your body in the gorge.
Among the Silk Roads and assassins,
you can scan a catalogue of automatics
and find what a bit more capital will buy.
The crime scene tape that flutters against
the tenement door, it understands you.
It whispers, *come, enter, make your notes,*
read the pattern on the playroom wall.
You're going to need all those drugs, to find
what bodies find when they are far away.

5.

Hallucination is a private room and all
the walls are fire. I learned that once.
Those days I was sleepless and neglected
to shave, and my arms in phantom pain.
Doctors wrote things down in files they
did not show me and said, *I see, well,*
that is all for now. So this is hell.
Never knowing where your choices end,
if the voice on fire is fire or the branch.
Or a summons to suffer what those deprived
of choices must. When I hear myself,
I am writing things down in files labeled,
That is all for now. And more simply,
all or *now.* Or *I have no heart to ask.*

6.

The window blinds cut a shadow lattice
across our faces, and as time withdrew,
our faces remained. Whatever the dragnet
pulled from the sea—call it water, whisper,
rope—it is all the great forgetting now.
Today, said the teacher, *we are learning*
about the world. Who here can find home.
Then she dizzied the globe, and I looked,
confused, and looked again. I searched the ocean,
name after name where it floated from shore.
True, the earth was changing. Nations flowed
into nations. Some grew. Others vanished.
I must have been somewhere down there,
but where I stood was nowhere to be found.

7.

Last night a ghost came to me and said,
a little terror haunts everything we do.
I do not think the voice talked to me
alone. Take any tower when it falls.
A refuse blooms, then it settles, fades.
Wounds harden. The urge to scratch becomes
its own problem, until that problem settles,
hardens. *Time heals*, we say. We say it again.
The children at their computers in class
look down, where the towers fall and fall.
They enter the cloud, the way light enters
the eye. It drags a bit of cloud-dust in,
no sooner felt than blinked into extinction.
The dead cannot hear you. Whatever they say.

8.

When my father was away in a coma,
I walked a lot, from midnight into dawn.
Fog rolled in. Smoke bloomed in TV
sets suspended from the hospital ceiling.
The world made a noise in the corner,
and as it grew, I grew. I searched the web.
We all did it. We made ourselves a part.
Compulsion had a cradle's rhythm, a pulse.
Open a page at dawn, and news rolls in.
I lived in two worlds then. My father in none.
When my nation burned, I played music
for the man. No one knew if he would
wake, if he heard us worry. Come back,
I whispered. It is beautiful here. Come back.

9.

Hell has its comforts, threnodies, charms,
But imagine what it takes to make
a life's work there, with only your powers
of invention to sustain you. Think
what you summons to complete the journey,
the blood and tears of your morbid desire.
I do not envy a creator that devoted,
divided, but here I am, on the edge
of the river. *A lighter craft will carry you,*
says the boatman, because I am that light.
I take his reasoning on faith. After all,
his Italian is so lovely, and the world so
full of weightless things, here a boat,
there a fly drinking from the open eye.

10.

A friend told me once, angel bodies
are made of *hearts*. *Harps,* she repeated,
they are made of harp, but I kept going
back to the sadder, funnier version,
heart sutured to heart, as testament
to the conviction of the needle and thread.
If I tell myself an angel cannot feel
what he is feeling, he becomes a puzzle
made of suffering with no one there
to suffer. If heaven is exclusion, it is
only human after all. Tonight
as I watch the election go south,
I too take refuge. I too share my blanket
with a cat, beside a fire that is dying.

11.

You can point your arrow at the head
of a god and click and read her story
in short form. The story of her story.
Your power is speed, so why waste it,
your wings synaptic, epileptic, seized.
You can leap from god to god, Jove
to Christ to Virgil. The links at the bottom
of the page say, *click me, no, me, me.*
If only you could click them all at once,
if your screen could multiply its cells,
you would see a pantheon, the pleas
for attention in small and smaller frames,
smaller gods. The surface of your eye
would break into a million, like a fly.

12.

The day I saw the Creation of Man,
the musculature of God reminded me
of lovers. Or if not love: cadavers,
the ones the painter loved to open up,
late, cutting deep into the parts quick
to yield and those that, heaven knows, were not.
He had to know what feeds, stabilizes,
links, how skin articulates what we
do not until we break it. I looked up
and saw the science underneath the art,
and I knew that I could always visit,
I could message the lord of the dead.
Just a touch of my finger, here, so ghost-
light, I cast no shade across the river.

13.

Dante says the suicides in hell
search in vain for the bodies they threw
away. So it is written, says the writer
to the soul for whom one life grew
inconceivable, one death unbearable
to the daughter he abandoned. If
design is cruel, what does it say about
us, the designers. I thank heaven
I was born to question, listen, choose
life and search for it in hell. Dante says,
suicides turn to trees because they fall,
when they fall, in the heart of the forest.
I know you, I say to the branches, I
loved you once. And looked for you in vain.

14.

The suicides in hell are beautiful,
their words music, their suffering unearthly.
I do not trust them, and still I read.
Through the effigies of steam, I see
smoke in mouths where there once there was
an explanation. I see a man, bent,
shivering in his chair in the garden,
the moment before he lay down there.
He had a son, friends whose last farewell
was anger. He had a stubborn god
and the one sin that has no time to be
redeemed. Forgive me, friends, I blame
no one. Not beauty, not you, not him.
Who am I to cast a stone. And where.

15.

When Dante looked up from the page
searching for a place to cast the souls,
his pen and the finger that it blackened
rose a moment, then he descended,
then his pen. It tore the man in half,
as paradise does when one feels lost
and longs to rise, and so to turn away.
Perfection made fools of his rivals,
a lion of his conscience, a jeweler's hammer
of the heart that beat his gold into submission.
He was proud, which is to say, alone,
afraid, and as he slept, face down, walking
into the world below, he curled a hand
below his chin, like an animal he loved.

16.

I balm my face in light that has no face,
and so I give it one, and so it says,
When I die, I want to be an ocean.
I want to be the snow that turns the skin
to rain, the rain to oceans, the ocean
to inconsolable angel. I want the sting
of that, the blush of anticipated seizure,
music and its end, that is a music still.
I want the emptiness where music lays
its harp and argument and glass. I want
to feel water thunder through my veins
with the joy that only thunder knows
and leaves and knows again, the knock
of halyards in the boatyard, dreaming of shore.

17.

Smoke rises in the theater dark,
so strong, this late, the movie is a blur,
but the bodies are out there, the cries
of bliss, the lamentations of the horn,
romances whose characters are tired
and give a new pantheon permission
to rise and fall against the broken shore.
Long ago I thought I needed pleasure
to survive love's withdrawal, to pull
out the sword of smoke and see the wound.
And then, in hell, I took my place on
the thwart beside a boy. I saw myself
in him. I saw him. I looked away. I
saw a shiver of stars on the vessel floor.

18.

The *spiritus mundi* of the modern age
bears the epithet of what we cast.
Less a *net* than an ocean, a nation
of no one, and yet the grave of all.
Our power is selection, so why waste it.
I think therefore I cast, I listen, I hear
the howl and siren and carnival tune,
the writhe of the catwalk and junkie,
the runaway child looking for connection.
I see the center that is everywhere,
the circumference that is nowhere,
not a god but the shape a god abandons.
I think, therefore I am a wave laid
in the waters that are a water's grave.

19.

If you believe the sermon in the distance,
the sorcerers in hell's torture chamber
lead a twisted life, heads on backwards,
buttocks blowing the trumpet of arrival
like the angel carved at the prow of a ship.
In other words, hell is funny, funny–
strange, funny-ha-ha, and thereby cruel,
if merciful, with anomalous reprisal.
Remember Simon Magus, how god-like
he flew, then Peter prayed, Simon fell
and suffered the fatal rocks of the crowd.
So magic works, just enough to kill,
if you fly, say, or pray a man to death,
or stoop to something equally inhuman.

20.

I saw once, in a cabinet made of glass,
a gold cross with a price on a string,
and I thought of the bones that informed
the spare design, the abstract of a man
deposed, suffering transcended. I thought
how inconsolable the joy whose parting
signature is loss. Once, a fish sufficed
as symbol of the faith, but then death cast
the wider net. When my father died,
wind broke the night into smaller pieces.
When we divided his things among us,
we divided. We grieved. We took home
fetishes, gifts, whose trace of him came
and went, like ecstasies of weather and gold.

21.

For the light of God is everywhere
equally distributed. Thus, the poet's
argument against greed. Tell me,
is it working. Fire flees the scene
of great suffering, and a cross remains.
The steady radiance is frightening.
Take this holy land. Is it working.
Or this ring whose diamond is undead.
The light at the end keeps flowing back
through cracks in the surfaces, prayers
in the rubble of the anointed temple.
The sacred falls upon its sword, again.
Everywhere the casket, the veil, the eyes
a child holds in darkness in her palms.

22.

Just as the bough sees its fallen garments
on the ground, so too the seed of Adam
descends to shore. The seed, says the poet.
And the garments of those who listen fall.
Any wonder lust is a largest circle.
When Narcissus drowned, he became
the flower that became the bee. He shook
the stinger as it dragged across his features.
He became no one apart from how
want is featured, in face and flower, to be
as two, made one, and therefore speechless, blind
as love for love in the largest circle.
When Narcissus drowned, he dove. So deep
the eye of the flower, there is no other.

23.

The Beatrice I love was the daughter
of a banker and married a banker in turn.
Dante met her twice, so she remained
a starlet, a narrative voice-over, a muse.
Her portrait hung in a golden ratio,
glassed in tears, as prized and policed
as the fountainheads of Florence, sweet
as parlor darkness bursting into honey.
An angel is not scary. It is lonely.
I have played this air guitar too long.
I have hung my head in a well so deep,
I floated my body out of my body.
Then a beautiful prospect came along.
Put this on, she said, *trust me, it's you.*

24.

Is it the same with you. Do you stare
down and see not home, but a place
you live, as gods live in heavens created
for our needs, before our needs evict them.
You cannot find him online: this man
beside his radio. The poem he recites
for a dollar is, each day, the same poem,
a rhyme about the moment, how this is
all there is. *Is,* he says again, with power.
One day chaos will find its home, as rain
that finds the vine, the verse, the cold red glass.
The man has promised to drink my dollar,
and I know, a poem like that is poison.
But here we are, each of us, a little late.

25.

I am listening to the pillow's heart,
the slow progress that it makes, and think,
Christ, I should give more cash away.
I should give, I should save, I should spend
my final years on gifts and medications.
Every day I pass the angel of my death
and feel ashamed. Is it better to look.
Or not look. I should know by now.
What is this rip in the common fabric,
if not a passage, the kind I hear when,
late, a window breaks in the basement,
and I have no basement, and why and where
a window. Is it better to wake or sleep.
To fall back, I wonder, as if to fall away.

26.

The creak of boats in swells of the harbor
sounds a warning like hinges of a forest
or failed estate. So difficult to get
the news from news, history from history,
by which I mean writing and the written
off. The auguries of smoke and wind
blow dust from the glass of eyes that sting.
Earth keeps spinning the storm surge north,
and mountains sink, and refugees come,
and foreign words for *home* in the distance
When a shoreline breaks, it breaks open,
and in flow the pixels too small to see,
stars of neither cruelty nor grace, but
a sorrow so deep its name has not arrived.

27.

I had a dream I fell deeper in dream,
and history called, but my phone rang
somewhere in a school cafeteria
late at night, no one there to answer.
The greatest poverty is not to live in
the physical world, said no one there.
I had that life where I belong to another
and I whispered *father?* like a stranger.
It could have been a poem about hell.
Or the deeper dream that objects dream
when they swear to you they will remember.
Given time, the stars of one paradise
fall hard against another, in the windows
lost to flood, ghosted by our eyes.

28.

When a high wind tears down the power
and it's you and me and the emptiness
that gives us license to move, we do not move.
We gather our cats in the pantry, we listen,
we hear in heaven the enormous sigh
of an iron lung exhaling, the storm eye
passing, the terrible burden coming to rest.
One part of every wind is trembling.
The other, the stillness the trembling moves aside.
The future, as we know it, is never true.
Never false. It is here in the quiet turn
of every breath, the little death a singer breathes.
One part of each departure is a mirror,
the other the wall to which a mirror turns.

29.

Panoptes, the god with a hundred eyes,
became a captive of the prison that bore
his name, the circle with guards in the center
and inmates on all sides who saw no one.
All that dark out there, and the hundred
fears to take a hundred points of view.
Why else does a man grow so many.
Misery, we know, is too much company.
Or too little. No one sees you, or no one
appears. When I see a prisoner in hell,
I see those eyes. I see a flock of grackles.
They break into the shrapnel of applause.
And then, nothing. I am alone. Just me
and a hundred sorrows. None of them, mine.

30.

Life, friends, is dangerous and dull
when it is not yours, and the moments
of some salacious or criminal betrayal
are small and smaller and easy to miss.
So why not hire a machine to watch
the machines, to harvest the enormity
of images and words we christen *terror.*
No Big Brother anymore, just a lot
of little people who are bored and listening
for a threat out there. And no doubt, soon
the agents will rest their heads on the keys.
The sleep they refuse will take them down
an inch, and they will learn to trust it, eyes closed,
to board the door that keeps our children safe.

31.

The affliction of the heretic is never
to see the world at hand, only a world
to come, and so the circle of the damned
whose every step is the one they are
not taking. I have been that man. I
drove so reckless I could have killed my friends.
I love, I said, and it was not love, but
a world without heresy is not the world
I forgive. Call it innocence or sin,
the volt of desire that could have killed us all.
The affliction of the fetishist is never
to reclaim our disbelief. I have been
that angel doused in gasoline, that eye
of the candle, the blindness of the flame.

32.

Back when I rented my books, I saw,
in the ledger pasted to the inner cover,
the signatures of students who carried
them before me. And there inside one,
I found the name of a famous assassin,
and it made me feel important, as he too
must have felt, for all the wrong reasons.
I touched the hand that touched the gun that touched
the better nation we might have been.
If I hated the man behind the name,
I did not feel it. I could not yet. I was
a star. *Today's lesson is about the power
of a name*, my teacher said. And so,
without warning, he took my book away.

33.

The photo of a man turns to the wall,
so weary of the gazing and the gazed.
That spirit of exchange you hear about
in poems, it cannot hear you. Poems go
to die in silence and in dirt. I hate that.
I hate it and honor it, whatever it takes
to pay attention. The greatest poverty,
I know, is idolatrous life. I could have
passed my suicidal friend in the street,
and I did not see him. If I gave a dollar
to my assassin, a *there-but-for-the-grace*
might have kept me from his eyes. A wind
could sweep the street of cigarettes, and I,
a dollar lighter, would shudder out of view.

34.

I was two boys then, and one, the older,
loved the monsters in fatality pictures.
Evil in the movies made sense in ways
history did not. Psychopathic criminals
looked away from the eyes of judges.
The rumored hand or handbag washed ashore.
Where once there was a character,
now there would be fate. Nothing more.
Where once there was trepidation, wonder.
Where once a beneficent god, a movie
called The Crawling Eye. And I pitied
that eye, shuffling slowly through the Alps.
I felt the cold against the iris, the sting
of heaven without shelter, blood, or tear.

35.

A friend taught me conviction is a nail.
When it meets its mark, it drags its
shadow in. Then he died, my friend.
Fuck-it, he says in the bar that I have
prepared for him, in the late-night talk
where I say, yes, fuck-it, and hate him
for it. If you search online, you can
find his home page still. His bio, his face.
His lamp is on, always burning. You
can look up My Death Space Dot Com
and read a cruel anatomy of failure.
If you are there, I want to ask. Is hell
a place where all your blunders follow you
into a hell where none of it matters.

36.

Why is it gods always talk in echoes,
if at all, their words buried in words.
Does it make them more important
than they are. Do they long to fill
an emptiness that must be empty still.
One day I will look for a friend's face
and see the words *this site does not exist.*
My double in this bar does not ask
about me. Who am I to blame him.
He cares less about the big picture
because he is one. He will tell you.
Hold an empty tumbler to your mouth.
See. It makes your voice a little larger.
Drink another. It makes you larger still.

37.

I am looking for a friend among us
in line for coffee, reading our phones,
and we bump bodies, and no one minds,
no one speaks to anybody here,
and still the more particular the death,
the more I see it in a stranger. I lay
a friend inside the chalk at the crime scene,
the way one lays a fire in the woods
or a child more deeply in the dream
she's in. One day I will turn a corner
and see no one, no song, no poem, no hat
to throw a dollar. Only Earth on fire,
and I will say I knew you, stranger, I will
ring your phone, weightless as an angel.

38.

When I was young, my teacher left the room,
and when she returned, she was not
my teacher, but a child. I did not know
enough to grieve, or to go wherever
a better child goes. I felt what I felt,
and mostly later, in the light of TV
faces that lined the streets of the republic.
I thought, so this is what a nation is.
What I felt, I heard in the soft drum
and the hooves of the cortege caisson
that bore the casket of our president.
My mother too watched. Perfectly still.
Until she called me and wiped something
from my cheek. A thing she never did.

39.

Blade after blade falls for a cause like heads
in a basket, and the spectacle leaves you
helpless, for the internet is no heaven,
no hell, no ethos. The guns have been printed.
The lonely are loaded. No one is alone.
The internet has no body to fuck or bury
or examine, no angel to bind your eyes.
It has no earth, no cancer, no rising sea.
Let me begin again. Long ago my teacher
left the room, and when she returned,
I saw no nation. I saw a woman in shock
do the best she could. Fragments, silence,
tears. I saw her struggle, her arms wrapped
around her chest where once there was a phantom.

40.

Long ago I died, and when I woke, deep
in the woods, dawn rose, and a white noise
in the radio clock with no clear station.
I was broken, like no other, into many
strangers then, and none of them was you.
Chaos has no face, and faces rise and fall
from it, like sunlight from a face we lose.
Long ago, I was torn from my younger,
older body, and a phantom pain poured
through. I was a radio. And it took years,
but then, one dawn, the pain felt distant, pale.
Strength returned. I woke, resolved, and tuned
to one clear song. And in the song, a tree,
bare and wingless, and capable of listening.

About The Author

Bruce Bond is the author of twenty-three books including, most recently, *Black Anthem* (Tampa Review Prize, University of Tampa, 2016), *Gold Bee* (Helen C. Smith Award, Crab Orchard Award, Southern Illinois University Press, 2016), *Sacrum* (Four Way Books, 2017), *Blackout Starlight: New and Selected Poems* 1997-2015 (E. Phillabaum Award, LSU, 2017), *Rise and Fall of the Lesser Sun Gods* (Elixir Poetry Prize, Elixir Press, 2018), *Frankenstein's Children* (Lost Horse Press, 2018) *Dear Reader* (Free Verse Editions, 2018), and *Plurality and the Poetics of Self* (Palgrave, 2019). Other honors include the Lynda Hull Memorial Poetry, Allen Tate, Laurence Goldstein Poetry, Richard Peterson, *River Styx* International Poetry, *New South* Poetry, and Meringoff awards, in addition to fellowships from the NEA and the Texas Institute for the Arts. Presently he is a Regents Professor of English at the University of North Texas.

Books from Etruscan Press

Etruscan Press Is Proud of Support Received From

Wilkes University

Youngstown State University

The Ohio Arts Council

The Stephen & Jeryl Oristaglio Foundation

The Nathalie & James Andrews Foundation

The National Endowment for the Arts

The New Mexico Community Foundation

Founded in 2001 with a generous grant from the Oristaglio Foundation, Etruscan Press is a nonprofit cooperative of poets and writers working to produce and promote books that nurture the dialogue among genres, achieve a distinctive voice, and reshape the literary and cultural histories of which we are a part.

etruscan press

www.etruscanpress.org

Etruscan Press books may be ordered from

Consortium Book Sales and Distribution

800.283.3572

www.cbsd.com

Etruscan Press is a 501(c)(3) nonprofit organization.
Contributions to Etruscan Press are tax deductible
as allowed under applicable law.
For more information, a prospectus,
or to order one of our titles,
contact us at books@etruscanpress.org.